save the . . .
FROGS

by **Sarah L. Thomson**
with an introduction
by **Chelsea Clinton**

PHILOMEL

PHILOMEL BOOKS
An imprint of Penguin Random House LLC, New York

First published in the United States of America by Philomel Books,
an imprint of Penguin Random House LLC, 2023

Text copyright © 2023 by Chelsea Clinton

Photo credits: page 4: © Chris Wellner/Smithsonian's National Zoo; page 7: © Matuty/
Adobe Stock; page 12: © Risto/Adobe Stock; page 17: © U.S. National Park Service;
page 23: © Buddy Mays/Alamy Stock Photo; page 33: © Solvin Zanki/Alamy Stock Photo;
page 38: © Peter/Adobe Stock; page 42: © David Northcott/Alamy Stock Photo; page 49:
© Star Tribune/Getty Images; page 52: © Mehgan Murphy/Smithsonian's National Zoo;
page 59: © Cecil W. Stoughton/U.S. National Park Service

Visit us online at penguinrandomhouse.com.

Library of Congress Cataloging-in-Publication Data is available.

Printed in the United States of America

ISBN 9780593404119 (hardcover)
ISBN 9780593404126 (paperback)

1st Printing

LSCC

Edited by Talia Benamy and Jill Santopolo
Design by Lily Qian
Text set in Calisto MT Pro

save the . . .

save the . . .
BLUE WHALES

save the . . .
ELEPHANTS

save the . . .
FROGS

save the . . .
GIRAFFES

save the . . .
GORILLAS

save the . . .
LIONS

save the . . .
POLAR BEARS

save the . . .
TIGERS

save the . . .
WHALE SHARKS

Dear Reader,

When I was around your age, my favorite animals were dinosaurs and elephants. I wanted to know everything I could about triceratopses, stegosauruses and other dinosaurs that had roamed our earth millions of years ago. Elephants, though, captured my curiosity and my heart. The more I learned about the largest animals on land today, the more I wanted to do to help keep them and other endangered species safe forever.

So I joined organizations working around the world to support endangered species and went to our local zoo to learn more about conservation efforts close to home (thanks to my parents and grandparents). I tried to learn as much as I could about how we can ensure animals and plants don't go extinct like the dinosaurs, especially since it's the choices that we're making that pose the greatest threat to their lives today.

The choices we make don't have to be huge to make

a real difference. When I was in elementary school, I used to cut up the plastic rings around six-packs of soda, glue them to brightly colored construction paper (purple was my favorite) and hand them out to whomever would take one in a one-girl campaign to raise awareness about the dangers that plastic six-pack rings posed to marine wildlife around the world. I learned about that from a book—*50 Simple Things Kids Can Do to Save the Earth*—which helped me understand that you're never too young to make a difference and that we all can change the world. I hope that this book will inform and inspire you to help save this and other endangered species. There are tens of thousands of species that are currently under threat, with more added every year. We have the power to save those species, and with your help, we can.

Sincerely,

Chelsea Clinton

save the . . .
FROGS

CONTENTS

1

ANYWHERE THERE'S WATER:
WHERE FROGS LIVE

Some endangered animals aren't easy to find. You probably won't spot a tiger in your backyard or a polar bear strolling down the street.

If you're looking for a frog, though, you're in luck. There are frogs and toads on every continent of Earth except Antarctica. Not every kind of frog or toad is endangered, but many of them are. You'll find out in chapter three why the world has become such a dangerous place for these small animals.

(What's the difference between a frog and a toad? Well, not much. A toad is just a kind of frog. Usually a toad has bumpy skin instead of smooth, and short hind legs instead of long. But there are some frogs with bumpy skin, and there are some toads with long legs—it just depends on the name given to that animal long ago.)

Frogs Worldwide

You'll find frogs pretty much anywhere with water. Swamps and ponds and streams are great places to look for frogs. But frogs can also live in forests, on mountains, and even in deserts and on the icy tundra where the soil deep underground is always frozen.

In the Arctic Circle, so far north that the sun

doesn't rise in the winter, you can find the wood frog. This amazing animal freezes nearly solid in the winter. It doesn't move. Its heart doesn't even beat. But it's not dead. It survives because its body replaces most of the water inside its cells with a kind of sugar. Water expands when it freezes. Sugar does not. So the sugar allows much of the frog's body to be frozen without harm. When spring arrives, the frog's body thaws, its heart begins to beat again, and it hops back off to its normal life.

In the warm, damp rainforest of Central and South America you might spot a poison frog. There are about 180 different species of these tiny frogs, and they are some of the most colorful animals on Earth. Their bright hues aren't just for show. They warn other animals that the frog's skin contains a liquid that can

The golden poison frog, which can be found in the South American country of Colombia, is one of the brightest and deadliest animals on Earth.

kill anyone who tries to take a bite—or at least make the predator sick. The golden poison frog is one of the most dangerous. It doesn't grow more than two inches long, but each little frog carries enough poison to kill ten people.

If you visit African rainforests near the equator, you might find the largest frog in the world: the goliath frog (also called the giant slippery frog). With a body eight to twelve inches long, it weighs more than a Chihuahua.

In the deserts of Australia, you could come across the water-holding frog. If you were very thirsty, that would be a good thing. During the rainy season, these frogs gulp down as much water as they can hold. When the rains stop, they burrow deep into the dirt to stay cool and moist. Their underground burrows are lined with many layers of the frog's own shed skin, which helps to keep the animal from drying out.

If you were lost in the desert and ran out of water, you could find a patch of mud and dig down to turn up a water-holding frog, then hold it over your mouth and squeeze. It would release the water it's holding, and you'd get a drink. The indigenous people of Australia have sometimes used these frogs as a source of water in an emergency.

In the jungles of Southeast Asia, you might look up at the trees and spot a Wallace's flying frog. These small green frogs are also called parachute frogs, and they have black webbing between their toes. When they jump from tree to tree, they spread their toes wide and also stretch out flaps of skin along the sides of their bodies. They can't really fly. (Only birds and bats can do that.) But Wallace's flying frogs can glide as much as fifty feet in a single leap.

You can find the common toad in most European countries, living in forests, grasslands, gardens, or under hedges, where they hunt for slugs and snails. In the spring, these small brown

Wallace's flying frogs, from the jungles of Malaysia and Borneo, spend almost all of their time in trees. The webbing on their toes acts like a parachute when they leap from branch to branch.

toads make their way back to the ponds where their eggs hatched. This can be difficult if they have to cross roads, so in parts of the UK, there are volunteers called Toad Patrols. They watch the places where toads are known to travel to

7

make sure they can get across the street safely.

And finally, if you live in North America east of the Rocky Mountains, you've probably heard a bullfrog. They don't measure up to the goliath frog, but they are the biggest frogs on the continent. Each can weigh as much as one pound. Hang out near the edge of a lake or pond or by a slowly moving river in the springtime and listen for the bellow of the male frog. It can be heard up to half a mile away.

No matter where frogs live—North or South America, Asia, Europe, Australia, or Africa—they need water to survive. That's because they are amphibians.

A Double Life

"Amphi" comes from an old Greek word that means "both." "Bian" comes from another word that means "life." So "amphibian" means an animal that lives a double life, both in water and on land.

There are three groups of amphibians: frogs, salamanders, and a rare snakelike creature called a caecilian. (You say it like this: see-CILL-yun.) All amphibians have backbones, or spines, and all are cold-blooded. That means that their body temperature is about the same as the air or water that surrounds them. Most amphibians are small, but not all. The biggest one, the Chinese giant salamander, can grow almost six feet long—longer than you are tall!

Amphibians have moist skin with no hair, fur, scales, or feathers. They draw oxygen into their bodies through that skin, and they soak up water the same way. If its skin dries out completely, an amphibian cannot survive.

Amphibians also need water for their soft, gooey eggs. Since the eggs don't have a hard shell like those of birds, they need water to keep them from drying out.

When an amphibian egg hatches, what comes out isn't a tiny frog or salamander or caecilian. It's something entirely different. That's because most amphibians, including frogs, have three-stage lives.

Frogs start out as eggs. They end up as frogs. But in the middle, they are something entirely different—tadpoles.

2

FROM EGGS TO TADPOLES TO FROGS: WHAT FROGS ARE LIKE

It's not just frogs—in fact, all animals begin life as eggs. In all mammals (except for the platypus and the echidna), the eggs stay inside the mother. That's where the baby grows until it is ready to be born.

All birds and almost all fish, insects, reptiles, and amphibians lay eggs that hatch outside of the mother's body.

That includes frogs.

Stage One—The Egg

Each year when the weather starts to get warmer, female frogs begin searching for some water where they can lay their eggs. If you go looking in ponds or streams or puddles in the spring, you might spot some. The eggs may clump together in a jellylike blob, spread over the water in a thin sheet, or cling to each other

Frog eggs are often clear with a black dot in the middle. The dot is what will turn into a tadpole.

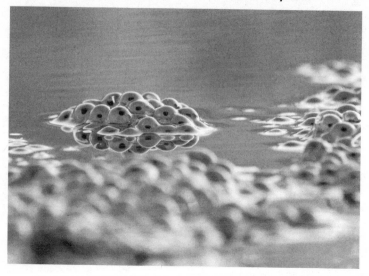

in long strings. (Some frogs lay one egg at a time that sinks to the bottom—you're not likely to see any of those.)

Some kinds of frogs lay a few hundred eggs at a time. Some lay thousands. Most of the eggs don't hatch, though. They may dry out, or they may get eaten. Just like a chicken egg might make a tasty breakfast for you, frog eggs make a good meal for almost any hungry predator. Fish, turtles, herons, and insects will all happily eat up a batch of frog eggs if they find them.

Once the female has laid her eggs, the male fertilizes them. Then most frog parents depart, leaving the eggs to their fate. But some frogs do stay close to protect their young.

A female glass frog lays her eggs underneath a rainforest leaf, gluing them in place with a glob of jellylike goo. Then she leaves, but her mate stays nearby. If a wasp comes to eat the eggs, the father kicks the intruder away with his strong back legs.

The tiny strawberry poison frog is bright red with blue back legs. (It's also known as the blue jeans frog.) The father watches over the eggs until they hatch, and then the mother takes over. She carries each tadpole to its own small puddle or pool and comes back every day to bring her young food. The food she delivers is her own eggs! The eggs she leaves for her tadpoles will not hatch. They're just meant to be eaten. And the mother is careful to only feed her own babies. She won't give an egg to tadpoles from another mother.

After the Surinam toad has laid her eggs, her mate nudges them onto her back, where they settle into her soft skin. Then an extra layer of skin grows over each egg. That's where the tadpoles hatch and develop into frogs—each in a tiny pocket beneath its mother's skin.

But it's the female gastric brooding frog of Australia (sadly now extinct) who might have found the safest place in the world for her eggs. She kept any predators from eating them by swallowing them herself. The eggs hatched inside her stomach, and later the baby frogs crawled out of their mother's mouth.

Stage Two—The Tadpole

When a frog's egg hatches, a tadpole squirms out. At least, that's true for most frogs. There are a few that skip the tadpole stage, like the Puerto Rican coqui. (You say it like this: co-KEY.) A tadpole is a larva—a young form of an animal that doesn't look or act at all like an adult.

Frogs aren't the only animal whose young have a larval stage. Think of a butterfly. It starts life as an egg and then hatches as a caterpillar (that's the larva). Later it hides inside a chrysalis to turn into a butterfly (that's the adult).

A larva might eat food that an adult wouldn't touch and live in a habitat where an adult couldn't survive. If you didn't know better, you'd think that the larva was another kind of animal entirely.

The larval, or tadpole, form of a frog must live in water. It takes in oxygen through its gills and uses a tail to swim. It looks a lot like a tiny fish, even though it's actually still an amphibian.

A tadpole has one main job—to eat. Tadpoles gobble up algae or plants or anything that was once living and is now dead and can be found floating nearby. Some will actually eat other tadpoles—living or dead. And some, like the strawberry poison frog or the Amazon milk frog, eat frog eggs.

Tadpoles need all of this food because they are growing fast, and because their bodies soon start to change.

First back legs grow from the sides of the tadpole. Then front legs sprout. Next the tail

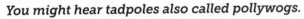

You might hear tadpoles also called pollywogs.

shrinks back into the body. The gills are covered with skin and, inside, the lungs develop.

Now the frog is an adult and in the last stage of its three-stage life.

Stage Three—The Frog

The change from larva to adult is called metamorphosis. For most tadpoles, metamorphosis takes a few months. For others, it's longer. American bullfrogs may take two years to turn from tadpoles into frogs.

Once a tadpole becomes a frog, how long does it live? We don't actually know how long most frogs survive in the wild. But in captivity, some have been known to live as long as twenty years.

Tadpoles are water-dwelling creatures, and so are some adult frogs. These frogs grow long legs with webs between their toes. The legs help them swim, and the webbing also pushes the frog through the water. (Have you ever worn flippers to swim? Those work a lot like the webbing between a frog's toes.)

Other frogs live mostly on land. They have shorter legs and their toes aren't webbed.

Some frogs walk or run instead of hopping. But many use their back legs for jumping, and frogs that do jump are champions at it. Some can leap up to twenty times the length of their own bodies. If you could do that, you could bound from third base to home plate in a single jump.

A frog may leap out of a predator's reach, but it doesn't use those powerful legs to travel great distances. Some kinds of frogs leave the pond or lake or puddle where they hatched, perhaps moving on to a nearby forest or meadow as an adult. They might return to the water to mate or lay eggs. A very wide-ranging frog might trek as far as nine miles in its lifetime, but that's pretty rare. Most frogs spend their lives close to home.

Sometimes that home is a steamy rainforest or a scorching desert. But for other frogs, home is a place where it gets cold in the winter.

You already know that frogs (like all amphibians) are cold-blooded. They can't stay warm if the air or the water around them gets cold. And most of them aren't like the wood frog of the Arctic—they can't let their bodies freeze solid and then thaw out in the spring. They have to find another strategy for surviving the cold.

That strategy is hibernation.

A frog will find or dig a sheltered burrow,

usually underground. Some frogs swim down to the mud at the bottom of a lake and stay there all winter long. It may get cold deep underground or underwater, but it doesn't freeze. It's like being in a refrigerator instead of in a freezer.

As it gets colder, a frog's body slows down, almost to a stop. The frog doesn't move. It barely breathes. It just waits until the snow and ice above it melt and the air grows warm again.

And when it wakes up in the spring, one of the first things it does is look around for something to eat.

A frog's eyes let it see in all directions (except for a little bit right behind them). That's handy for spotting prey. Most tadpoles may eat a bit of whatever they find in the water, but all adult frogs are carnivores. They don't eat plants. Instead, they hunt other animals. Insects, spiders, snails, worms, fish, and sometimes small mammals, birds, reptiles, or other frogs may wind up as a meal for a hungry frog. One scientist found a goliath frog with a bat in its stomach!

After a frog spots prey, it opens its mouth. The tongue flips out. In less than a second, the end of the tongue snags a flying insect or some other nearby prey.

You've probably heard that the end of a frog's tongue is sticky, but that's not exactly true. The frog's tongue is actually soft rather than sticky—much softer and squishier than your own tongue. And it's wet. The wet, soft, squishy tongue slathers saliva all over its prey.

Then the tongue folds back up, heading for the mouth. As the tongue moves, something remarkable happens to that saliva. It becomes as thick as honey. The prey cannot get loose.

The frog's tongue has snagged a moth for a meal.

As soon as the tongue is completely inside the mouth, the frog gets ready to swallow. To do that, it has to close its eyes. The eyes pull back inside the head and press down on the roof of the mouth, squishing the tongue and the struggling prey. That pressure makes the saliva thin and slippery again, and the prey slides off the tongue and down the frog's throat.

Frogs don't chew their meals. They gulp down the mouthful whole. Once the food has been swallowed, the frog's eyeballs pop back out and open as the frog looks for something else to eat.

Just behind its eyes, you can find a frog's ears. But they're not easy to spot. They look like patches of flat skin with nothing that sticks out. Those flat ears are excellent at hearing, which is a good thing, because many frogs can make a lot of noise. Most of the sounds a frog makes are to call to a mate or to warn other frogs away.

Male frogs are usually the loudest. Many of them have a vocal sac in the throat, which they fill with air so that it bulges out like a balloon. This sac is a bit like a microphone. It picks up the sound from the frog's vocal cords and

And sometimes frogs themselves are the invaders, which is what happened in Australia in the 1930s.

Sugarcane beetles were a problem in Australia. As you probably figured out from their name, they like to eat sugarcane. Farmers wanted to find a way to get rid of the pesky beetles. It seemed like a great idea to bring in cane toads to eat them. A few hundred toads were brought to a town in Queensland and set free.

It didn't turn out the way people had hoped. Cane toads do not eat sugarcane beetles. But they do eat just about everything else, including native frogs.

And a female cane toad can lay up to thirty thousand eggs at a time. Even if they don't all hatch (they don't), that's still a lot of tadpoles to grow into new cane toads that eat and eat and eat some more.

And what eats the cane toads? Not much. Cane toads are poisonous, even when they are tadpoles. Any predator who eats one does not survive to eat another. An Australian mammal called the northern quoll is now on the Red List as Endangered. One likely cause is that these small predators try to eat cane toads and end up dying.

Cane toads eat insects, snails, snakes, other frogs, and the eggs of birds that build their nests on the ground.

Since they were first released, cane toads have spread across much of northern Australia. The Australian government has tried to control them by fencing off ponds to keep the frogs out and by encouraging people to remove eggs from the water and to catch and kill adult toads. But the truth is, there's no way to find all the eggs or nab all the toads. Cane toads are in Australia to stay. And there is a real risk that they will drive many local animals (including other frogs) to extinction.

Nowhere to Live

The American bullfrog might be able to survive chytrid fungus, but it (along with many other frogs) faces different problems. One of the biggest is the loss of its habitats, the places it can live.

All frogs, remember, need at least a little bit of water. Many thrive in damp places—marshes, swamps, ponds, streams, creeks, and lakes.

But there are 7.8 billion people on the planet. And our numbers keep growing. We take over more and more land, putting up houses and stores and other buildings, and laying down sidewalks and roads and railroad tracks. All of this means that frogs have less wetland to live in.

Sometimes people decide to leave a pond or a stream alone when they build. But that might not be enough to help. Frogs often travel away from their water source to find food and return to it to lay eggs. If a road is in the way, many frogs get killed by traffic before they can reach the water.

And even if they get safely to the water, other problems may be lurking.

What's in the Water?

In August of 1995, ten seventh and eighth graders from the Minnesota New Country School in Le Sueur, Minnesota, were on a field trip to the nearby Ney Nature Center. The pond was full of leopard frogs, but as the students began catching one slippery amphibian after another, they realized that something wasn't right. Some frogs had deformed legs. Or extra legs. Or legs that were missing entirely. Some had missing eyes. Some had twisted spines. Something was very wrong with the frogs in this pond.

The kids returned to school and posted pictures of the frogs on the school's website. Reports of deformed frogs in other places began to turn up—some from Minnesota, others from all over the world. It seemed that frogs everywhere were hatching with misshapen legs,

This American bullfrog was born with six legs and will never be able to walk or hop normally.

missing eyes, and serious problems with the organs inside their bodies.

What was happening?

Even today, more than twenty-five years later, people are still not sure. But most scientists think that the problem is in the water.

Tadpoles grow up in water. Frogs soak in

water through their skins. If the water isn't clean, it's going to affect the frogs.

When farmers and gardeners spray pesticides on their plants to kill insects, some of those pesticides get washed off by rain and dew. They sink into the ground. From there they can trickle into small creeks and streams, which flow into larger rivers and ponds and lakes. Pesticides can also evaporate into the air with water and fall again later as rain.

The same thing happens when people spray herbicides to kill weeds. Farmers also spread fertilizer on their crops to help them grow, and some of that fertilizer gets washed into nearby water sources as well.

Chemicals from factories end up in the water. When we scrub a sink or toilet or bathtub, the cleaning products get washed down the drain. Drains lead back to lakes and ponds and rivers where frogs and other animals live.

As frogs soak up water through their skins, they soak up anything that gets put into that water. This makes frogs into something called an indicator species.

An indicator species is one that is easily affected by the environment around it. If an indicator species starts to get sick or die off, it is a sign that something is very wrong with something in its environment—maybe the water, the air, or the soil. We need to quickly figure out what the problem is, or it will spread.

Luckily, a lot of people are trying to figure out what is wrong with frogs—not just in Minnesota, but all over the world.

4

KIDS, SCIENTISTS, ACTIVISTS, AND DOGS: WHO HAS BEEN SAVING FROGS?

Who would want to live in a world with no frogs hopping in the grass? No tadpoles wiggling in ponds or puddles? Frogs are fascinating and fun—and they're also very important to the environment they live in.

Many other animals—from herons to snakes to otters to humans—rely on frogs for food. If frogs vanish, these animals could be in trouble.

Frogs eat as well as get eaten, and a lot of

them eat insects. If there were no frogs to keep insect populations in control, people (and other animals and plants too) would suffer.

And people studying frogs hope to make a lot of new discoveries, like the one made by scientists studying the phantasmal poison frog. The liquid that oozes from this frog's skin can be made into a powerful painkiller. There may be other frogs out there who can help scientists find more new medicines—but this can only happen if there are still frogs around to study.

And finally, since frogs are an indicator species, we need to pay especially close attention when they are in trouble. Saving frogs is good for the frogs, of course. And it can also be good for other animals, for plants, and for human beings as well. That's because the same problems that affect frogs now will affect other species later, unless we take action.

Kids and Scientists

Remember the seventh and eighth graders at the Minnesota New Country School, the ones who raised the alarm about the deformed leopard frogs at the Ney Nature Center? The kids' teacher reached out to a scientist, Judy Helgen, who worked at the Minnesota Pollution Control Agency. Helgen wanted to learn more about what the students had discovered. She talked to the kids, studied frogs in the pond, and went to nearby farms to learn more about what was happening.

According to Helgen, the people in charge at the Minnesota Pollution Control Agency began to discourage her from continuing her research.

She believes that they didn't want her to find out if chemicals from nearby farms were leaking into the pond's water and harming the frogs—perhaps because that kind of news would not be welcome to the farmers. Six years after the schoolchildren had found their first deformed frogs, the Minnesota Pollution Control Agency stopped the study, even though they still weren't sure exactly what was happening to the frogs.

By that time Helgen was ready to retire. She was unhappy to be leaving without finding out the answer to what was happening to the frogs in Ney Pond and elsewhere. But as she visited the pond one last time, she felt comfort in thinking that there were many others who would keep working to solve the mystery. She thought of kids who were just beginning to learn about the natural world and all its fascinating creatures, frogs included. Perhaps some of those kids would grow up and help finish the work that she had started.

She was right. The work *did* continue. Scientists all over the world are still trying to understand what causes problems for frogs like the ones in Ney Pond. It isn't a simple problem, and more work remains to be done.

Judy Helgen holds a leopard frog taken from Ney Pond. This frog was lucky enough to develop normally.

Helgen was also right in thinking that there were kids who would grow up to take on the work of caring for the natural world. One of the students from the Minnesota New Country School—Becky Pollack—did just that. She had been on the field trip where the deformed leopard frogs were discovered. She grew up to become the executive director of the Ney Nature Center, working hard to keep the pond and its surroundings as a safe, clean habitat for leopard frogs and many other animals.

Project Golden Frog

In the 1990s, scientists realized that the Panamanian golden frogs were dying.

These tiny, bright yellow frogs are a symbol of the Central American country where they live, just as the bald eagle is a symbol of the

United States. The frogs, or little statues of them, are thought to bring good luck and good fortune.

Researchers scrambled to figure out what was happening. Fairly quickly they realized that chytrid fungus, which damages the skin of frogs and other amphibians, was killing the golden frogs. And time was running out.

Project Golden Frog, or Proyecto Rana Dorada, was launched.

No one knew (and still no one knows) how to get chytrid fungus out of streams and ponds. So they decided to get the frogs out of the streams and ponds instead.

First scientists studied the remaining wild frogs to figure out exactly what they would need to survive in captivity. By the year 2000, people working for Project Golden Frog were

Researchers and volunteers are hoping to keep the Panamanian golden frog alive until it is safe to return them to the wild.

ready to capture frogs and ship them to zoos in the US and Canada.

No one has seen a golden frog in the wild since 2009, but zoos have more than 1,600 of them. As the frogs lay eggs and tadpoles hatch, the population grows. Scientists are still trying to find ways to clear chytrid fungus from the water in the frog's natural habitat. When that happens, they can be released into the wild again. Until then, Project Golden Frog will keep the species from extinction.

The San Diego Zoo and the Frog Dogs

Yellow-legged frogs that live in the San Jacinto Mountains of California were facing many threats. Trout that had been brought to the area were eating them. Droughts, when not enough rain fell, meant it was hard for the frogs to find water. Chytrid fungus was killing them. The species was in trouble.

Rescuers found eighty tadpoles in a drying creek bed and brought them to the San Diego Zoo's center for conservation research. Scientists tried to figure out the best way to help the tadpoles grow into healthy frogs. They learned what the frogs preferred to eat, when to keep the lab chilly to encourage them to hibernate, and how to turn the lights in the lab on and off at the right times. This meant that the frogs would get the same amount of light as they would if they lived in the wild.

At last the center had enough frogs to try releasing some back into the mountains. But they needed a way to keep track of the frogs and make sure they survived.

When scientists are trying to find and count a population of wild animals, they sometimes use traps, but this wouldn't work for frogs. They're too small and could be hurt in a trap.

Sometimes scientists hike out to the animal's habitat and look for them, counting as many as they can see. But yellow-legged frogs like to hide under rocks and in cracks between boulders. They're hard to track by sight. Sometimes scientists listen to the calls that animals make—but yellow-legged frogs make very little noise.

So some scientists have tried implanting small radio transmitters under the frogs' skin or putting the transmitters in little frog-sized backpacks. The transmitters let out a signal that the scientists could use to track the frogs down. Other scientists tried a different method of tracking released frogs. They called on the help of the Frog Dogs, also known as the Amphibian Research K9 Team.

The first Frog Dog was Luna, a mixed-breed dog (a mutt) born in Mexico. By the summer of 2020 there were four more Frog Dogs: a Chihuahua mix called Bighetti, a hound mix named Niko, a border collie known as Flynn, and an Australian shepherd, Darby.

A trainer taught the dogs to follow the scent of yellow-legged frogs. When a dog found a frog, they got a reward—maybe some steak, a hot dog, or a toy to play with. Soon they became experts.

The Frog Dogs can track frogs in all sorts of wild landscapes. Bighetti, the smallest Frog Dog, can fit into a backpack to be carried up steep hills and alongside waterfalls where the other dogs have trouble keeping up. The bigger dogs with their longer legs can easily hike for miles to distant sites where frogs might be hiding.

The sharp noses of the Frog Dogs are a big help when it comes to tracking down yellow-legged frogs and discovering if the species can still thrive in the wild.

Clean Water for All

In 1969, many people were beginning to realize that water pollution was a serious problem.

In that one year, pollution from factories in Florida killed 26.5 million fish in Lake Thonotosassa. An oil spill in California turned beaches black and killed thousands of birds. And the Cuyahoga River in Ohio caught on fire.

Yes, a *river* caught on *fire*. There was so much oil floating on the surface of the water that it burst into flames. It wasn't the first time, either. The Cuyahoga was so polluted that it had been on fire at least nine times before—maybe more.

Water pollution is terrible for humans, plants, and animals alike—and of course it's particularly bad for frogs and other amphibians. At all stages of their three-stage lives—as eggs, tadpoles, and adults—frogs must have clean water to survive.

As the 1970s began, environmental groups, activists, and ordinary people began to speak up, demanding new laws and better protection from pollution. They insisted that everyone in America—from humans to fish to frogs—had a right to water that wasn't full of trash, polluted with chemicals, or actually *on fire*.

In 1970, the very first Earth Day was celebrated. Twenty million people gathered to ask the government to do more to protect the environment. That same year, the US government created the Environmental Protection Agency (or the EPA) and gave it the job of making rules that would safeguard the natural world.

In 1972, the US government passed a law called the Clean Water Act.

Protestors like these at the first Earth Day in 1970 put pressure on the US government to pass laws protecting the environment.

This law gave the new EPA power to set limits on many kinds of water pollution. When factories and other polluters dump filthy water right into rivers and lakes and ponds, the EPA can force them to stop.

Since the Clean Water Act, lakes, ponds, rivers, and streams in the US have been much cleaner. It's estimated that, by itself, this act keeps 700 million pounds of pollution out of American waters every single year, leaving that water cleaner for tadpoles, frogs, and all the other living things that depend on it to survive.

The act was a big step forward, but there is still more to be done. Groups like the Natural Resources Defense Council, the Sierra Club, and the Nature Conservancy haven't stopped working. Along with a lot of everyday people who phone and write letters to lawmakers and get together in big groups to call for change, they continue to push for laws that will keep Earth's water clean.

One of those people is Autumn Peltier.

Born on Manitoulin Island in Lake Huron, Peltier is a member of the Wiikwemkoong First Nation. She began to fight for clean water at an early age. When she was just twelve years old, she had a chance to meet the prime minister of Canada, Justin Trudeau, and she told him in straightforward words how she felt. "I'm very disappointed in the choices you've made," she said to him, urging him to do more to make clean water available to everyone.

Three years later, at fifteen, Peltier spoke at the United Nations in New York City, reminding global leaders that all life depends on clean water. "I've said it once, and I'll say it again: we can't eat money or drink oil," she warned them. That same year, she was appointed the Anishinabek Nation Chief Water Commissioner.

With people like Peltier and others fighting for clean water for all, endangered frogs and many other animals still have a chance to survive.

SOME FUN FACTS ABOUT FROGS

1. The glass frog has transparent skin on its stomach. You can see its bones, muscles, stomach, and heart from the outside.

2. Horny toads are not toads at all. They're not frogs, either. They are actually lizards.

3. The marsupial frog keeps her eggs in a pouch on her belly, a lot like a kangaroo. When the tadpoles hatch, she opens the pouch with her toes and lets her babies swim free.

4. North American spadefoot toads spend a lot of their time underground. But they

come out of their burrows to mate when it rains in the summer, sometimes hundreds at a time. They all croak together, a sound that some people think sounds like "rain today, rain today."

5. The Budgett's frog sometimes screams if it feels threatened.

6. The longest recorded jump that a frog ever made was at a frog-jumping contest in South Africa. The winner, named Santjie, jumped thirty-three feet and five and a half inches. Santjie could easily have jumped across a two-lane road in a single leap.

7. Frogs shed their skin about once a month. They twist and stretch to loosen the old skin, and then pull it over their heads, very much like you'd peel off a

tight sweater. The frog will often eat the dead skin.

8. Some frogs can change color. They may go from dark to light or the other way around when they are excited or alarmed. The arum frog, native to South Africa, lives inside lily flowers. It is white while the lilies are blooming, but turns brown when the flowers wilt and turn brown themselves.

9. Glass frogs keep their eggs from drying out with urine. In some species the mother pees on the eggs. In others it's the father's job.

10. Not all frogs croak. Some use other methods of communication. The Panamanian golden frog waves its front legs to attract the attention of other frogs.

This way of communicating is called "semaphore."

11. A group of frogs is called an army.

12. The red-eyed tree frog lays its eggs on leaves that hang over water. When the eggs hatch, the tadpoles fall into the water and swim away.

13. Some frogs have teeth, even though they don't chew their food. If a species has teeth, their teeth are usually very small and only in the upper jaw. They help to keep prey from escaping out of the frog's mouth.

HOW YOU CAN HELP SAVE THE FROGS

1. Frogs, like other amphibians, need water, places to hide, and something to eat. If you and your family have a backyard, you can provide all of these things for frogs with a pond. Here's some advice on how to make one: PlanetPatrol.info /frogpond.html.

2. Even if you can't make your own pond, you can make your yard a friendly place for frogs and other small creatures by leaving dead leaves or logs in some spots. Frogs can use these as hiding places.

3. Don't leave litter or trash around bodies of water. (Or anywhere, really.) Frogs need clean water to survive. Other animals do too. If you see some litter, carefully pick it up and get rid of it in a trash can or a recycling bin. (You can keep a plastic bag with you and use it to protect your hands.)

4. Organize a cleanup day near a pond or stream. If your family, some friends, or your class at school all pitch in, you'll get a lot more done.

5. Keep your dog on a leash while walking near streams or in marshes or meadows. A dog who loves to dig can disturb frogs and other amphibians.

6. If you are going on a trip where you will be camping or hiking around lakes,

streams, or ponds, check online to see if there is chytrid fungus in the area. If there is, wash your clothes and clean off any camping equipment when you get home. Wipe off your shoes with some Lysol or a combination of bleach and water. It's very important not to spread chytrid fungus to new places.

7. Learn even more about how amazing frogs are. You can visit a zoo or an aquarium and see living frogs. Check and see if the place you want to visit has been approved (or accredited) by the AZA—that's the Association of Zoos and Aquariums. (You can learn more about them at AZA.org.) If it has, that means that the animals there are getting the best care possible.

8. You can also check out these books to learn more about frogs:

The Case of the Vanishing Golden Frogs: A Scientific Mystery
by Sandra Markle

The Mystery of Darwin's Frog
by Marty Crump

From Tadpole to Frog
by Wendy Pfeffer

9. Don't dump motor oil or cleaning chemicals down the drain. They may end up in ponds, lakes, and rivers where frogs live. Instead, go online and search "hazardous waste disposal" and your town's name to find out how to get rid of these things safely.

10. Try to use as little water as possible at home. This will leave more water in ponds, streams, and lakes for frogs and other wild creatures. Take quick showers, turn off the water while you scrub your hands or brush your teeth, and run the dishwasher only when it's full.

11. Never bring a frog or another amphibian from one body of water to another. This is the main way chytrid fungus spreads. Never release a pet frog or other amphibian into the wild.

12. Ask your parents not to use pesticides (which kill bugs) or herbicides (which kill weeds) in your yard. They do more than get rid of bugs and weeds. They also kill frogs and other amphibians and poison the water where these animals live.

13. Your yard will need less herbicides and

pesticides (and less watering too) if it is full of native plants. Native Plant Finder at NWF.org/NativePlantFinder is a great place to research which plants are right for your area.

14. Donate some money to an organization like the National Resources Defense Council, the Nature Conservancy, or the Sierra Club, which work to preserve wetlands and water sources for all wild creatures. Need some ideas for ways to raise money? Check out AmphibianArk .org/Support-Us/Fundraising-For-Kids for some possibilities.

15. Frogs are the animal most commonly used in science classrooms for students to dissect. Not all frogs sold to classrooms are caught in the wild, but many are, and taking frogs from ponds or streams can be bad both for the frogs and the environment they live in. If your school (or the school you'll go to when you're older) has students dissect frogs, you can ask the science teachers or the principal to think about other choices. Students can dissect model frogs or learn from computer programs rather than dissecting real animals.

REFERENCES

"About Frogs." Mass Audubon. Accessed
September 3, 2021. massaudubon.org
/learn/nature-wildlife/reptiles
-amphibians/frogs/about.

ActiveWild.com Admin. "Wallace's Flying
Frog Facts, Pictures, Video, and In-Depth
Information: Discover an Amazing
Gliding Frog." Active Wild, July 2, 2018.
activewild.com/wallaces-flying-frog.

American Museum of Natural History.
"Frogs: A Chorus of Colors." Exhibitions:

Past Exhibitions. May 18, 2018. amnh.org
/exhibitions/frogs-a-chorus-of-colors.

BioKids. "Green Frog." Bio Kids: Critter Cata-
log. The University of Michigan. Accessed
September 3, 2021. animaldiversity.org
/accounts/Lithobates_clamitans.

Bittel, Jason. "Half of All Amphibian Species
at Risk of Extinction." *National Geographic*,
May 8, 2019. nationalgeographic.com
/animals/article/more-amphibians-at
-extinction-risk-than-thought.

"Blue Jeans Poison Dart Frog." CostaRica.
com. Last updated: June 17, 2015.
costarica.com/wildlife/blue-jeans-poison
-dart-frogs.

Boissoneault, Lorraine. "The Cuyahoga River
Caught Fire at Least a Dozen Times, but

No One Cared Until 1969." *Smithsonian Magazine*, June 19, 2019. smithsonianmag.com/history/cuyahoga-river-caught-fire-least-dozen-times-no-one-cared-until-1969-180972444.

Butler, Tina. "Cane Toads Increasingly a Problem in Australia." Mongabay, April 17, 2005. news.mongabay.com/2005/04/cane-toads-increasingly-a-problem-in-australia.

The Canadian Press. "'We Can't Eat Money or Drink Oil': Indigenous Teen Autumn Peltier Tells United Nations." *Canada's National Observer*, September 29, 2019. nationalobserver.com/2019/09/29/news/we-cant-eat-money-or-drink-oil-indigenous-teen-autumn-peltier-tells-united-nations.

Curtis, Michelle. "Frog Dogs." Science Blog. San Diego Zoo Wildlife Alliance, June 8, 2020. science.sandiegozoo.org/science -blog/frog-dogs.

"Frogs: The Thin Green Line: What You Can Do to Help the Frogs." *Nature.* PBS, August 9, 2012. pbs.org/wnet/nature /frogs-the-thin-green-line-what-you-can -do-to-help-the-frogs/4842.

Gallant, David Joseph. "Autumn Peltier." *The Canadian Encyclopedia.* Historica Canada. Last modified October 25, 2021. thecanadianencyclopedia.ca/en/article /autumn-peltier.

Helgen, Judy. *Peril in the Ponds: Deformed Frogs, Politics, and a Biologist's Quest.* Amherst, MA: University of Massachusetts Press, 2012.

of Nature (IUCN) keeps track of animal species all over the world. Their Red List of Threatened Species™ puts each animal in one of these categories:

Least Concern: This animal is doing all right. There are enough healthy animals to have enough healthy babies to keep the species going.

Near Threatened: This animal is not in trouble yet, but there are danger signs. It may become Vulnerable, Endangered, or Critically Endangered soon.

Vulnerable: There are not many of this animal left, its numbers are falling, and it can live only in certain small areas. It is at risk of extinction.

Endangered: This animal is at *high risk* of extinction.

Critically Endangered: This animal is at *very high risk* of extinction.

Extinct in the Wild: This animal lives only in captivity. There are no wild ones left.

Extinct: This animal is gone forever.

The gastric brooding frog, which swallowed its eggs and let them hatch safely in its stomach, was last seen in the wild in the 1980s. It is considered Extinct. The goliath frog is Endangered. The Panamanian golden frog is Critically Endangered and may not exist in the wild anymore. In the next chapter, you'll find out what people are doing to save this tiny, bright yellow frog that is a symbol of the country where it lives.

Other species are doing better. The strawberry poison frog and the American bullfrog are of Least Concern. But many frogs are in trouble all over the world.

Why are frogs having such a hard time surviving?

A sawmill owner is said to have carried about a dozen trout in a coffeepot to a creek near his mill in 1876. Other explorers, miners, and prospectors of the time did the same thing, hoping to fill troutless lakes with fish they could later catch and eat.

It worked. The trout thrived in their new home. Later, as fishing for fun became more and more popular, the government took over the work of making sure that there would always be plenty of trout to catch. Today, the Department of Fish and Wildlife brings truckloads of young trout to the lakes of the Sierra Nevada.

All those trout need something to eat, and they are happy to dine on the local animals, including the Sierra Nevada yellow-legged frog. It wasn't long before more than 90 percent of the frogs had been wiped out.

that is not naturally found in a particular area is called an introduced species. If it does a lot of harm in its new home, it may be called something else—invasive.

Sometimes people bring a species to a new place by accident. An insect that has burrowed into a log might be carried to a new state or country in a load of lumber, for example. Or a weed might travel from one lake to another stuck on the propeller of a boat.

Other times people bring a species to a new place on purpose. Like trout.

The highest parts of the Sierra Nevada mountains in the western United States had sparkling lakes and bright streams—but no trout. And people like catching and eating trout, so they began to bring trout to the mountains and set them free.

A Deadly Fungus

You know how important a frog's skin is. If the frog's skin isn't healthy, the frog can't be healthy.

A deadly threat to frogs' skin is lurking in waters all over the world. It's called chytrid fungus. (You say it like this: KIE-trid.)

A fungus looks a lot like a plant, but there's one big difference. A plant can make its own food directly from sunlight, but a fungus cannot. It has to grow on and take its food from another living thing.

Maybe you've seen mushrooms growing on trees or logs. These are a kind of fungus, and they take the food they need from the wood of the tree. Athlete's foot is a kind of fungus that grows on human skin (particularly between the toes). It gets its food from the skin it lives on.

Chytrid fungus is similar. It grows on the skin of frogs and other amphibians.

Tiny bits, or spores, of the fungus float in the water of streams, ponds, and puddles where frogs spend a lot of their time. If a spore settles on a frog, it sinks small tendrils, like roots, into the frog's skin. These tendrils give off chemicals that break the skin down. The fungus then takes in parts of that skin as food for itself.

A frog with damaged skin gets weak and sick. After a time, it may die.

When a frog that is infected travels to a new pond or pool, spores of the fungus break off to float in the water and infect others. So one frog might spread chytrid fungus to a nearby pond . . . and a second frog might catch it there and spread it to a stream . . . and so the fungus will move slowly across the landscape.

A researcher examines a Tyrrhenian painted frog infected with chytrid fungus.

People speed up this process by catching frogs in one place and bringing them to another. American bullfrogs are often caught and sold for food, since people enjoy the taste of frog legs. Bullfrogs can catch chytrid fungus, but they usually don't get sick or die from it. However, they do carry the fungus with them

wherever they are sold, bringing it to new places where it can infect new frogs.

Something similar happened with African clawed frogs. More than sixty years ago, these frogs were caught in southern Africa and shipped all over the world because scientists used them in laboratory experiments. Many clawed frogs were infected with chytrid fungus, and so the fungus spread.

When chytrid fungus comes to a new place, it can kill so many frogs that entire species vanish. We already know that chytrid has driven ninety different species of amphibians to extinction. Many more are at risk of dying out forever.

You Don't Belong

Frogs aren't the only animals that people move from one place to another. A plant or animal

makes it louder—much louder. When the coqui frog of Puerto Rico calls out "co-KEY, co-KEY," one little frog can be as loud as a lawn mower.

What's on the Outside Matters

From head and ears to toes, frogs are covered by a soft, moist skin. That skin does more than just protect the frog from dirt or injury.

You already know that frogs breathe through their skin. They have lungs, just like you, but they must also soak up oxygen from the air or the water around them. As long as their skin stays soft and moist, that's what they do.

A frog also soaks up water through its skin. They don't use their mouths to drink. Its skin is the only way for a frog to get the water it needs.

And another kind of liquid oozes the other way, from inside the frog's body to the outside

of its skin. This liquid is poisonous. In most cases, the poison isn't strong enough to kill or even annoy a predator, and certainly not strong enough to harm a human being.

But toads do release a milky-white fluid from behind their eyes that burns or stings the mouth and eyes of anything that tries to eat them. (If you pick up a toad, be sure to wash your hands afterward. You wouldn't want to rub any of this goop into your eyes.) And the poison frogs of South and Central America use their bright colors to warn predators that the liquid in their skin is deadly. Anyone who tries to eat one of these frogs will regret it.

If a frog can't poison a predator, it might try to hide from it instead. There are many animals that would love to make a tasty meal out of a frog—turtles, snakes, fish, herons,

raccoons, otters, and minks are just a few.

That's one reason why so many frogs are green or brown or a combination of both. These drab frogs are well camouflaged among leaves, grass, reeds, mud, or rocks. Some frogs, like the long-nosed horned frog, have triangular points over their eyes and snouts that look like the edges of leaves. Ridges along their backs look like the leaves' veins. If these frogs stay still, they are almost impossible to tell apart from the leaves in their forest homes.

So a frog's skin has many lifesaving jobs— soaking up oxygen and water, helping the frog hide, or warning predators away. But a frog's skin is also delicate. Anything that damages a frog's skin can put that frog at risk.

3

POLLUTION, FUNGUS, AND INVADERS: WHY ARE FROGS ENDANGERED?

Scientists have discovered somewhere between seven and eight thousand species of amphibians. (There are probably more that we haven't found yet. Many amphibians are small and very good at hiding.) More than half of those amphibians are frogs.

And between one-third and one-half of all amphibians on Earth are at risk of extinction.

The International Union for Conservation

History.com Editors. "The Clean Water Act Becomes Law." HISTORY. A&E Television Networks, April 7, 2020. history.com/this-day-in-history/clean-water-act-becomes-law.

"History of Minnesota New Country School." Minnesota New Country School. Accessed August 18, 2021. newcountryschool.com/page/mncs-history.

Lyden, Tom. "Un-Frog-getable: What Happened to Minnesota's Deformed Frogs?" FOX 9, May 9, 2021. Updated May 10, 2021. fox9.com/newsun-frog-getable-what-happened-to-minnesotas-deformed-frogs.

Markle, Sandra. *The Case of the Vanishing Golden Frogs: A Scientific Mystery.* Minneapolis, MN: Millbrook Press, 2012.

Mianecki, Julie. "14 Fun Facts About Frogs."
Smithsonian Magazine, June 20, 2011.
smithsonianmag.com/science-nature
/14-fun-facts-about-frogs-180947089/.

Minnesota Pollution Control Agency. "Frequently Asked Questions about Deformed
Frogs." Living Green. Accessed August 12,
2021. pca.state.mn.us/frequently-asked
-questions-about-deformed-frogs.

Nat Geo Wild. *The Glass Frog: Ultimate Ninja
Dad: Animal 24.* National Geographic.
July 3, 2017. YouTube video, 2:36.
youtube.com/watch?v=U7zARByAu1c.

National Aquarium. "American Bullfrog."
Accessed September 1, 2021. aqua.org
/explore/animals/american-bullfrog.

National Geographic. "Amphibian Pictures
and Facts." Animals. Accessed August 12,

2021. nationalgeographic.com/animals
/amphibians.

National Geographic Kids. "The Frog Life
Cycle!" Discover: Science. Accessed
August 12, 2021. natgeokids.com/uk
/discover/science/nature/frog-life-cycle.

National Geographic Kids. "Wacky Weekend:
Frogs." Accessed August 12, 2021. kids.
nationalgeographic.com/wacky-weekend
/article/frogs.

National Wildlife Federation. "This Leap Year,
Frogs Are Leaping for Their Lives." The
National Wildlife Federation Blog. Accessed
August 16, 2021. nwf.org/~/media/PDFs
/Global-Warming/Frog-Leap-Day-Fact
sheet.ashx.

Nuwer, Rachel. "A Small Band of Panamanian
Golden Frogs Is Saving Their Species from

Oblivion." *Smithsonian Magazine*, April
2021. smithsonianmag.com/smithsonian
-institution/small-band-panamanian
-golden-frog-saving-species-oblivion
-180977151.

Project Golden Frog. Accessed August 17,
2021. proyectoranadorada.org/index.php.

San Diego Zoo Wildlife Alliance. "Frog and
Toad." San Diego Zoo Wildlife Alliance:
Animals and Plants. Accessed August 1,
2021. animals.sandiegozoo.org/animals
/frog-and-toad.

San Diego Zoo Wildlife Alliance. "Goliath
Frog." San Diego Zoo Wildlife Alliance:
Animals and Plants. Accessed September
1, 2021. animals.sandiegozoo.org/animals
/goliath-frog.

San Diego Zoo Wildlife Alliance. "How We're

Helping to Save the Mountain Yellow-
legged Frog." Science. Accessed August
19, 2021. science.sandiegozoo.org
/species/mountain-yellow-legged-frog.

Tesler, Pearl. "The Amazing Adaptable Frog."
Frogs. The Exploratorium, February 13,
1999. exploratorium.edu/frogs/mainstory.

The Wildlife Trusts. "Common Toad." Wildlife Explorer: Amphibians. Accessed
September 1, 2021. wildlifetrusts.org
/wildlife-explorer/amphibians/common
-toad.

Wolfe, Warren. "Deformed Frogs Still a
Mystery." *Star Tribune* (Minneapolis, MN),
September 13, 2012. startribune.com
/deformed-frogs-still-a-mystery/169510776.

SARAH L. THOMSON has published more than thirty books, including prose and poetry, fiction and nonfiction, picture books, and novels. Her work includes two adventures featuring a teenage-girl ninja, a riveting survival story about wildfires and wombats, and nonfiction about elephants, sharks, tigers, plesiosaurs, saber-toothed cats, and other fascinating creatures. *School Library Journal* called Sarah's picture book *Cub's Big World* "a big must-have." *The Bulletin of the Center for Children's Books* described her novel *Deadly Flowers* as "clever, dangerous, vivacious," and *Booklist* said this fantasy set in feudal Japan is "genuinely thrilling, with surprises at every turn and a solid emotional core." *Deadly Flowers* also received Wisconsin's Elizabeth Burr/Worzalla award. Sarah worked as an editor at HarperCollins and Simon & Schuster before becoming a full-time writer. She lives in Portland, Maine.

Learn more about her work at
SarahLThomson.com

CHELSEA CLINTON is the author of the #1 *New York Times* bestseller *She Persisted: 13 American Women Who Changed the World*; *She Persisted Around the World: 13 Women Who Changed History*; *She Persisted in Sports: American Olympians Who Changed the Game*; *Don't Let Them Disappear: 12 Endangered Species Across the Globe*; *It's Your World: Get Informed, Get Inspired & Get Going!*; *Start Now!: You Can Make a Difference*; with Hillary Clinton, *Grandma's Gardens* and *The Book of Gutsy Women: Favorite Stories of Courage and Resilience*; and, with Devi Sridhar, *Governing Global Health: Who Runs the World and Why?* She is also the Vice Chair of the Clinton Foundation, where she works on many initiatives, including those that help empower the next generation of leaders. She lives in New York City with her husband, Marc, their children and their dog, Soren.

You can follow Chelsea Clinton on Twitter
@ChelseaClinton
or on Facebook at
Facebook.com/ChelseaClinton

DON'T MISS MORE BOOKS IN THE

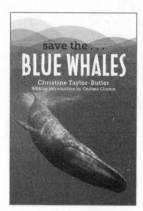